P9-CQG-405

The Story of
SPYING

Rob Lloyd Jones

Designed by Karen Tomlins

History consultant: Terry Charman

Reading consultant: Alison Kelly, Roehampton University

Illustrated by Ian McNee
Edited by Jane Chisholm

First published in 2007 by Usborne Publishing Ltd,
Usborne House, 83-85 Saffron Hill, London EC1N 8RT, England.
www.usborne.com

Internet links

You can find out more about the world of espionage by going to the
Usborne Quicklinks Website at www.usborne-quicklinks.com and
typing the keyword 'Spying'. The recommended websites are
regularly reviewed and updated but, please note, Usborne Publishing
is not responsible for the content of websites other than its own.

Contents

Chapter 1

Secrets and spies

F ar above the earth, satellites glide through space. Some record weather data, others receive telephone signals. But a few are on more secret missions. Armed with incredibly powerful cameras, spy satellites photograph enemy warships and army camps, beaming the images to secret agents below.

Spy agencies guide satellites like this
to snap long-range photographs
over enemy territory.

Today, the art of obtaining secret information about an enemy – known as spying, or espionage – is filled with sophisticated technology and high-tech gadgets. But spies have been operating unseen and undetected for more than 2,500 years.

The jagged, rocky peaks of the Indus Valley, in India, were perfect for Alexander the Great's spies to hide among, watching enemy armies in secret.

The Ancient Greek king Alexander the Great created a network of secret agents to ride ahead of his army and watch enemy troops from the hillsides. In case they were caught, the spies wrote messages to each other in secret codes that their enemies couldn't read.

Spymaster Sir Francis Walsingham, shown
in the portrait above, was one of Queen
Elizabeth's most trusted minsters.

As more and more European nations fought
in wars against each other, each developed
organized networks of secret agents, or spy
rings, to keep watch over their enemies. Many
of these spy rings were very well trained, run
by individuals known as spymasters.

During the 16th century, one of the first spymasters, Sir Francis Walsingham, was obsessed with protecting the English queen Elizabeth I from enemy plots. Walsingham even formed a special spy school, teaching over 50 agents how to intercept and decode secret letters, fake an enemy's handwriting, and send invisible messages. These were written in milk or lemon juice, which could be read when the paper was warmed over a candle.

Walsingham's greatest spying success came in 1586, when he uncovered a conspiracy to assassinate Queen Elizabeth. At the heart of the plot was the Queen's cousin Mary, Queen of Scots.

At that time, Mary was in jail for supporting the Queen's enemies. Walsingham hated her, so was delighted to discover a secret letter she had attempted to smuggle from jail hidden inside a beer barrel. The letter seemed to order Queen Elizabeth's death, although many now believe Walsingham forged it himself to make Mary appear guilty.

When she saw the evidence in court, Mary was outraged. "Spies" she protested, "are men of doubtful credit, who make a show of one thing and speak another."

The judge wasn't moved, and Mary was executed on February 8, 1587.

This 19th century painting shows Mary, Queen of Scots being led to her execution. Many people believe she was framed by spymaster Sir Francis Walsingham.

As well as trained spies, many spymasters also employed artists as secret agents. Artists were useful because they moved from city to city working on different paintings, so were able to watch enemy activity without suspicion.

At the start of the 16th century, artist Leonardo da Vinci worked for a wealthy Italian nobleman, drawing landscapes for his army to use when they planned their military campaigns.

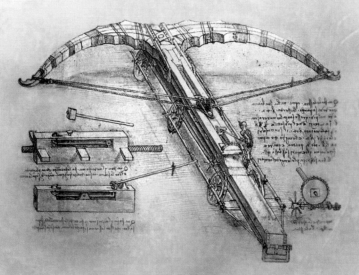

Leonardo da Vinci also designed weapons, like this huge crossbow, for the armies of Italian nobles.

Later, other artists – such as the Dutch painter Willem van de Velde the Elder – were employed to sketch ships in enemy docks. These drawings were sent home and studied to work out the vessels' weaknesses.

By the 18th century, espionage was common in North America, too. From 1775 to 1783, the American Continental Army fought the British in a war of independence. Their commander and chief spymaster, George Washington, was always one step ahead of his enemies.

Often, British spies thought they had intercepted Washington's secret orders, when in fact they had been planted by the spymaster to spread false information – or disinformation – about the strength and location of his troops.

This 18th century painting shows the American Continental Army, on the left, in battle against British troops.

Almost a hundred years later, the United States was torn apart by a civil war fought between the northern and southern states. Virginia hotel owner Belle Boyd hated the northern, or Union, army, because they had once attacked her mother's house. When their soldiers occupied her town, she seized the opportunity to spy on them for the southern forces, known as the Confederates.

Wearing fancy dresses and feathers in her hat, she mingled with the Union soldiers in bars, charming them into divulging secrets about their army's activities. She even eavesdropped through secret holes in the walls of their hotel rooms.

This photograph shows Belle Boyd dressed to impress the army officers she was spying on.

Belle Boyd's hatred of the Union army began when Union soldiers raided her home, shown here, in Martinsburg, West Virginia.

Whatever secrets Belle discovered, she wrote down and hid inside an old watchcase. She then rode through the night to deliver them to the Confederate camp.

By the time she was twenty-one, Belle had been arrested seven times, and sent to prison twice. But she always managed to talk her way out – and once even convinced a prison guard to marry her. After the war, she toured America, giving dramatic accounts of her amazing exploits in espionage.

On the other side of the world, spies were busy during a struggle between Britain and Russia for control over the mountains and deserts of Central Asia. This area lay strategically between the Russian empire and the British empire in India, and the contest, which lasted over 50 years, became known as 'the Great Game'.

Both sides sent army officers to the region on missions to make secret alliances with local rulers. This was dangerous work. Agents had to climb through perilous mountain passes to reach towns that were suspicious of foreigners. The spies used false names, or arrived disguised as cattle traders.

In 1838, British Army officer Charles Stoddart reached the region of Bukhara, hoping to gain the ruler's support against Russia. But Stoddart knew little about local customs, and accidentally insulted the ruler by staying on his horse when he approached his palace. He was hurled into a dank dungeon crawling with insects.

A year later, another British agent, Arthur Conolly, came searching for Stoddart – but he too was tossed into the dungeon. The pair remained there for two terrible years. When they were taken out, they were stick-thin and covered in sores. The two spies were dragged to the town square, forced to dig their own graves – and then beheaded.

During the Great Game, British agents often trekked over icy mountain passes like this to spy on enemy activity.

Chapter 2

In the line of fire

A thick fog wrapped around the Tower of London on the morning of November 6, 1914. A door creaked open, and guards led German spy Carl Lody towards a rifle range, where a firing squad was waiting to execute him. Strangely, the guards seemed more nervous than the prisoner. Lody simply stared up at the clouds, breathing deep lungfuls of the cold, crisp air.

As the guards led him forward, he turned to a British officer and smiled. "I don't suppose", he asked, "you would care to shake the hand of an enemy spy?"

The officer hesitated, then accepted Lody's outstretched hand. "No," he replied, "but I will shake hands with a brave man."

Moments later, a volley of gunfire echoed around the Tower's old walls. Carl Hans Lody was dead.

Carl Lody was one of eleven German spies executed at the Tower of London during the First World War. These agents had been sent to Britain on surveillance missions – to listen to and watch the enemy, gathering as many secrets as possible.

Throughout history, dozens of spies have been imprisoned and executed here, at the Tower of London.

All Carl Lody needed to spy on British military bases was a notepad and a pair of binoculars.

Disguised as an American tourist, Lody toured England, Scotland and Ireland, collecting information on British military bases. Often, he rode past them on a bicycle, scribbling secret notes, then sending the information to Germany disguised as letters to his friends.

Unfortunately for Lody, the British Secret Service intercepted most of his secret letters. He was arrested in October 1914, and immediately sentenced to death.

Shortly before his execution, Lody wrote a last letter to his family. "A hero's death on the battlefield is certainly finer," he told them, "but such is not to be my lot, and I die here in the Enemy's country, silent and unknown..."

This photograph of Carl Lody was
taken after his arrest in 1914.

Like Lody, most German agents were given
false names and backgrounds, known as cover
stories, to hide their real identities. One
agent, Carl Muller, arrived in Britain
disguised as a tourist, and sent several reports
back to Germany during his stay. These
reports looked like innocent postcards, but
they contained invisible messages written in
lemon juice.

Another group of German agents in Britain pretended to be salesmen, sending secrets home disguised as orders for cigars from British seamen. The spies, though, had planned badly, and didn't know that British sailors preferred to smoke pipes. They were quickly caught when their letters were intercepted by the secret service.

One of the most famous spies of the First World War was Margaretha Zelle, an exotic dancer who called herself Mata Hari. Margaretha was from the Netherlands, a neutral nation in the war, so she could move freely across national borders to work in nightclubs all over Europe. Appearing on stage in glamorous costumes, she attracted the attention of men wherever she went.

One of these men was a senior German army officer named Karl Kramer. Margaretha mingled with so many powerful military men, Kramer thought she would make an ideal spy. He asked her to work for him in secret, and even gave her a special code name – H-21.

Margaretha had grown bored with her life, so spying seemed like a new adventure. The problem was, she had also agreed to spy for the French secret service – *against* the Germans. Drinking and dancing with army officers, she picked up scraps of information and reported them back to both sides.

To her, espionage was just a delightful game.

Mata Hari's exotic dancing in nightclubs earned her the attention of many senior military officers.

But to the French secret service it was deadly serious. Since Margaretha had given them no useful information, they became suspicious that she was double-dealing. The Germans lost patience with her too. While Margaretha was on a mission in Spain, they deliberately leaked information to the French, naming her as a German spy.

Margaretha was arrested as soon as she returned to France, and executed for espionage. She had been a bad spy, but she showed great courage before her death, refusing to wear a blindfold in front of the firing squad. She is even said to have blown the riflemen a kiss just before they fired.

Mata Hari was executed by a French firing squad on October 15, 1917.

British spies in France often had to sneak past guard posts like this.

Chapter 3

Behind enemy lines

"Halt!" The German guard's rifle shook in his hands as he aimed it at the woman approaching his checkpoint. "Identify yourself!" he yelled.

It was 1943, the middle of the Second World War. The German army had conquered most of Europe, invading Poland, Belgium, and now France. But, in France particularly, many people were still fighting against them. German troops had been ordered to watch for anything suspicious.

"Open your bag!" the guard shouted.

Calmly, the woman held the satchel open. Inside sat an electronic device covered in wires. The guard jumped back, scared it was a bomb. But now the women opened her satchel wider, pointing to her blue nurse's uniform. Had the guard not seen an X-ray machine before, she asked.

The soldier stared at the machine for a moment, then nodded her on, pleased to have done his job. But he had been tricked. The machine was a radio in disguise, and the nurse was a British secret agent.

At that time, the Germans were preparing to invade Britain from France. Desperate to stop them, the British army created an elite force, known as the Special Operations Executive (SOE), to work deep in enemy territory. Their mission was to cause as much damage as possible through acts of sabotage, such as destroying German tanks or blowing up their weapons stores. The British Prime Minister, Winston Churchill, ordered them to, "set Europe ablaze."

SOE agents were recruited from all sorts of backgrounds. Some were former soldiers, but others were journalists, electricians, or even taxi drivers. All of these men and women underwent a gruelling training course at secret locations across the British countryside.

Among other skills, they were taught how to trail enemies undetected, break into enemy bases, parachute into enemy territory, and remain disguised while they were there. These disguises included false moustaches and fake scars. Some agents even had plastic surgery to change their appearance between missions.

SOE agents were dropped behind enemy lines at night, when they were less likely to be seen.

SOE agents were also trained to use a variety of weapons and explosives, such as guns fitted with silencers and special 'garrotting' wires, which they used to creep up and strangle guards from behind.

They were then given ingenious gadgets to use on their missions, including false tree trunks that contained radio equipment, toothpaste tubes with secret chambers, and silencers to attach onto the ends of their guns. One of the strangest weapons, though, was a dead rat filled with dynamite, which SOE agents secretly placed near enemy campfires. When German soldiers threw the dead animal into the flames, it exploded.

By the end of the war, in 1945, over 10,000 SOE agents had been sent on secret missions – not only in Europe, but also to Africa and the Far East. They derailed trains, blew up bridges, and sank ships. They even assassinated important German army officers. No one knew where they would strike next, and only 200 SOE agents were ever captured.

SOE agents were trained to use explosives to attack enemy targets.

Many of the captured agents were interrogated by the German secret police force, the Gestapo, and forced to send false information to their headquarters in Britain. But the SOE was ready for this; agents usually sent messages home using deliberately misspelled words – when they were captured, they simply spelled the words correctly. That way, SOE controllers in London knew something was wrong.

One of the SOE agents caught by the Gestapo was a young woman named Violette Szabo. Before she became a secret agent, Violette worked in a department store in London. Her husband, a French army captain named Etienne, was away fighting in North Africa. Every day, Violette prayed he would return home safely.

Violette Szabo poses with her husband
Etienne, whose death led her to join the SOE.

Then, in 1942, she heard that Etienne had been killed. Heartbroken, Violette became determined to get involved in the war herself.

"My husband has been killed by the Germans," she told her friends, "now I'm going to get my own back."

Violette spoke perfect French and was skilled with a rifle, so she was ideal for dangerous missions behind enemy lines. The SOE recruited her immediately.

Violette was sent on two operations to France, working with rebel French soldiers fighting the Germans. On her second mission, in 1944, she was ambushed by a German army patrol and trapped in a terrible shootout. Before she was captured, it is said that she managed to kill several German soldiers and help other SOE agents to escape.

Violette now suffered a terrifying fate: interrogation, torture, and imprisonment in a concentration camp. The Gestapo were desperate for her to reveal secrets about her fellow agents. But, through it all, she refused to tell them anything about the SOE. Frustrated, the Germans finally executed her in the spring of 1945.

After her death, Violette Szabo was awarded medals for bravery from both the French and the British governments.

Chapter 4

The Enigma code

Locals in the sleepy English village of Bletchley watched with disapproval as several cars passed their houses in August 1939. Word had spread that an army captain was having a party at Bletchley Park, a country house just outside the town. At that time, war clouds were gathering over Europe, so it seemed wrong that these military men and women should be out having fun.

But as the cars pulled up beside the old Victorian mansion, none of the passengers were smiling. They weren't here for a party at all. They were on one of the most classified missions of the Second World War: to crack the German army's secret codes.

Since the 1920s, the Germans had been sending secret radio messages to each other using devices called Enigma machines. These machines looked like typewriters, but contained several small cogs that scrambled any words typed into them by an operator. To unscramble the message, the cogs on the receiver's machine had to be set in exactly the same sequence. If not, the words came out as a confused jumble.

Since there were over 150 million million million possible ways the cogs could be set, the Germans thought their code was unbreakable. But in fact it already had been broken. In 1933, French and Polish spies discovered the sequence of the Enigma machine's cogs, and deciphered several secret German radio transmissions.

But, as war approached, the German grew even more concerned about the secrecy of their communications, so began changing the cog sequence every single day. Now the code really did seem impossible to crack.

German soldiers are photographed here using an Enigma code machine to send classified messages.

Even so, the British army's Code and Cypher School was determined to try. If they succeeded, they would be able to eavesdrop on their enemy's greatest secrets. They chose Bletchley Park as the headquarters for this new mission, and recruited some of the country's top brains as code breakers: chess champions, language experts, and award-winning mathematicians. In total, there were 200 operatives, all sworn to absolute secrecy. Even Bletchley Park itself was given a secret name: Station X.

Code breakers at Bletchley Park worked for hours in tiny huts like this on the mansion's lawns.

Bletchley Park was surrounded by gardens, where code breakers relaxed between long shifts at work.

Each day, the code breakers at Station X received as many as 3,000 coded German messages, which had been intercepted at special listening posts, known as Y Stations, located across Britain.

The code breakers worked day and night in little huts erected on the mansion's lawns, comparing each new message with the others. They hoped to find a pattern that would reveal how the Germans had set the Enigma machine's cogs that day.

One of the cleverest code breakers at Bletchley Park was a mathematical genius named Alan Turing. In 1940, Turing designed a huge decoding machine, known as a bombe, which used motors to search through all the possible Enigma cog settings.

A member of the Women's Royal Navy is photographed here operating a bombe machine at Bletchley Park.

It was an amazing success. Soon, patterns began to emerge from the coded jumbles ...then words ...then whole messages.

Now agents at Station X could read all sorts of secrets about the German forces. They could help their navy guide

Alan Turing, inventor of the bombe decoding machine that helped crack the Enigma code

ships away from enemy submarines, the army could avoid ambushes, and the air force could keep control of the skies. When Prime Minister Winston Churchill learned about the discoveries at Bletchley, he called the code breakers, "the geese that laid the golden eggs."

Far from the blood and bullets of the battlefield, the brainy code breakers at Bletchley Park played a major role in the outcome of the Second World War.

Chapter 5

Deceit and double-cross

After the Second World War ended in 1945, a new rivalry emerged between the Soviet Union and the USA. The two countries had very different political and economic systems, known as communism and capitalism. Neither side trusted the other, and they built powerful nuclear weapons to protect themselves.

After the Second World War, the city of Berlin, in Germany, was divided into capitalist and communist sections by this long guarded wall.

This period of hostility, which lasted for over fifty years, became known as the Cold War, because there was little actual fighting between the two sides. Instead, the soldiers of the Cold War were spies.

During the Cold War, both the United States and the Soviet Union built vast spy networks to keep watch on each other. In America, the Central Intelligence Agency, or CIA, ran secret, or covert, operations to overthrow enemy communist leaders.

Europe during the Cold War

Norway
Sweden
Finland
SOVIET UNION
Moscow

United Kingdom

East Germany
Poland
West Germany
France
Yugoslavia
Italy
Spain
Turkey

Capitalist nations

Communist nations

Neutral countries

The map above shows how Europe was divided between capitalist and communist nations during the Cold War. The boundary was known as the 'Iron Curtain'.

In the Soviet Union, the largest intelligence agency was the Committee of State Security, better known by its Russian initials, KGB. The KGB's preferred spy technique was infiltration – finding enemy agents who would betray their country by stealing secrets. These spies were known as moles, because they dug their way unseen into enemy organizations.

The Soviets often organized grand parades like this to show off their military strength.

Senior CIA officer Aldrich Ames knew how much the KGB paid moles for stolen secrets. He was heavily in debt, and needed the money badly. In April 1985, Ames walked into the Soviet Embassy in Washington D.C. and handed over an envelope. Inside were names of two KGB officers who worked undercover for the Americans. In return, the KGB gave him another envelope – stuffed with $50,000 in cash. From that moment, Ames was addicted.

Here, crowds watch Soviet missiles pass beneath a banner of Lenin, their former leader.

This secret FBI surveillance photograph
shows US agents arresting enemy spy
Aldrich Ames in 1994.

Over the next nine years, Ames sold the
KGB names of at least 25 more American
agents working in the Soviet Union, as well
as details of more than 100 covert CIA
operations. He had little care for the
consequences. He even betrayed some of his
own best friends, who were then captured and
killed by the KGB. In total, the KGB paid
Ames over $2.7 million for his treachery.

Ames bought a new car, a new house, and began taking expensive trips abroad. He even paraded around CIA headquarters in stylish new suits. But, as more and more American agents went missing, the CIA grew suspicious of Ames's new wealth.

The FBI began following him everywhere, and photographed his secret meetings with the KGB. Ames was finally arrested in 1994 – but by then he'd become the most damaging spy in CIA history.

Ames betrayed his country for money, but other agents did so because they believed it was the right thing to do. Soviet army general Dimitri Polyakov was convinced that a communist government would destroy the Soviet Union, so he agreed to work as a mole for the CIA for almost 20 years. When the CIA offered him a home in the USA to repay him for his efforts, he refused.

"I am not doing this for you," he told them, "I am doing this for my country."

Another celebrated Soviet military hero, Oleg Penkovsky, also refused to accept payment for spying for the West. Penkovsky was convinced that the Soviet government was leading the world towards a nuclear war. He believed he could stop them by giving details about their bombs to their enemies.

These spy cameras and films are similar to those used by Oleg Penkovsky to photograph secret Soviet documents.

From 1961 to 1962, he photographed over 5,000 secret files about Soviet missiles, then smuggled the films to the British intelligence agency, MI6. Penkovsky knew the KGB might be following him, so he was very careful about how he delivered the stolen secrets.

On one occasion, Penkovsky visited a Moscow park where the wife of a British intelligence officer, Janet Chisholm, waited with her three young children. Penkovsky was then able to pass camera films to the children hidden inside bags of sweets.

The KGB finally caught Penkovsky in 1962, and executed him for spying. To them, he was a traitor, but the British and Americans regarded him as the most important spy of the Cold War.

Janet Chisholm, shown here with her children, met Oleg Penkovsky in a Moscow park close to where they lived.

Chapter 6

Spy science and fiction

On the morning of September 7, 1978, Bulgarian journalist Georgi Markov crossed a bridge on the River Thames, in London, heading for a nearby bus stop. It was a journey he made every day to get to work. But as he stood waiting for the bus, Georgi felt a sudden, stabbing pain in his leg.

Glancing back, he saw a man rushing away from him carrying an umbrella. Had the man just jabbed him with it? Rubbing his leg, Georgi boarded the bus and thought little more about the incident. But he should have – the man was a KGB-trained assassin, and his umbrella was a poison gun. Three days later, Georgi Markov was dead.

Crowds like this on London's bridges helped Georgi Markov's assassin escape undetected.

The KGB's umbrella gun was one of many spy gadgets, known as sneakies, invented during the Cold War. The KGB killed Georgi Markov because he spoke against communism on the radio, but most sneakies were created for secret surveillance.

The most common were bugs, mini listening devices small enough to hide almost anywhere. In 1946, the Soviets gave American diplomats in Moscow a wooden sculpture to hang in their embassy. The Americans thought it was a gesture of peace, but later discovered it contained a bug to listen in on their secret meetings.

In response, the CIA tried to spy on the Soviets by planting a bug inside a live cat. Sadly, the animal died on its first mission – when it was run over by a car.

Other sneaky surveillance tools used during the Cold War included special glasses to help agents see in the dark, cameras that took photographs by detecting body heat, and powerful microphones that could pick up conversations over 100m (around 300ft) away.

Most of the KGB's secret operations were planned here, in the Soviet capital of Moscow.

U-2 spy planes like this flew so high that the pilots had to breathe pure oxygen through special helmets.

To spy from even further away, new planes were designed, such as the U-2 spy plane, which could fly from New York to Moscow non-stop at over 21km (around 13 miles) above the earth. Like satellites, these planes could survey vast areas of territory beneath them to search for enemy bases.

The existence of U-2 planes was meant to be a secret. But in 1960, an American U-2 was shot down while on a spying mission over the Soviet Union. The pilot, Francis Gary Powers, confessed to being an American spy, but the CIA insisted the plane had been conducting an innocent weather experiment.

The US navy also sent submarines on spying missions. These boats roamed the waters close to the Soviet Union, searching for telephone cables carrying secret enemy messages. When they found one, divers walked along the seabed and tapped into the line. They could then listen into the enemy's deepest secrets.

Crews of Cold War submarines like this were sworn to absolute secrecy about their missions.

These underwater operations were so secret, even the crews didn't always know where they were going. They were incredibly dangerous, too. If a submarine became stuck on the seabed, the Soviets would know they had been spying. For such emergencies, the captain was trained to use special explosives – destroying the submarine and killing his crew.

The CIA also developed new ways to conceal stolen information. Microdots were tiny blocks of information written in code and reduced to the size of a pinhead. They could then be hidden behind a postage stamp, for instance, or even in a dental filling. Once the microdot had been delivered, it could be decoded and read using a microscope.

Perhaps, though, the most sophisticated piece of spy technology developed during the Cold War was the Cray-1 supercomputer. This machine could solve over 100 million mathematical equations every second, and crack almost any code. Today, the CIA uses a similar computer, which can solve an incredible 2.4 *trillion* equations per second.

Other incredible inventions of the Cold War included guns disguised as key chains, cigarette cases, and even tubes of lipstick (a weapon the KGB called the 'Kiss of Death'). But since so little is known about sucessful spy missions, it's hard to tell how often these gadgets were ever used.

It is known, though, that the CIA once tried to kill the communist president of Cuba, Fidel Castro, by leaving an exploding seashell on a beach where he swam. When that didn't work, they tried to humiliate him instead, by sprinkling a powder in his shoes that would make his beard fall out. But that failed too.

Fidel Castro, the communist leader of Cuba, laughs at a newspaper story about a plot to assassinate him.

ve One Blackout Puzzle -- Win $14,250

Journal American AFTERNOON EDITION

All Police on Alert

OT TO KILL CASTRO!

Sinister devices like these have been made famous by spy novels and films, like those about British MI6 agent James Bond. Many of these stories glamorize the life of spies, making them seem foolhardy and reckless. In fact, the best agents are much more careful and calculating. They all know that one tiny mistake could lead to their capture, imprisonment, and even execution. Even so, some real-life agents have acted with almost as much cool as James Bond.

This poster for a James Bond movie is typical of the glamorous way spies are portrayed in fiction.

Soviet super-spy Konon Molody spent seven years in Britain living under a false identity, stealing secrets about the Royal Navy. When the police finally arrested him in 1961, he simply smiled and asked if there was someone he could play chess against in jail.

Konon Molody,
Soviet super-spy

Molody was one of the Soviet Union's top spies, and so he knew he would eventually be traded in an exchange for a British spy in a Soviet prison. He was right – three years later he returned to the Soviet Union to a hero's welcome.

Today, companies, as well as governments, use espionage to keep track of their enemies. This is known as industrial espionage. It can be as high-tech as hacking into another company's computers, or as simple as searching their waste bins for sensitive documents. Some companies have even used bribes and blackmail to steal secrets from their competitors.

Often, industrial espionage is used to discover details about a rival company's products – new car designs, for example, or computer systems. A company can lose vast sums of money if its plans are leaked, so many now have tight security measures to stop this from happening.

Even away from the shadowy world of espionage, most of us are being spied on in one way or another. In some cities, the streets are watched by CCTV (closed-circuit television) cameras that record your every move. Although they're designed for our protection, some people find them intrusive – proof that there are few places left where someone's not watching you.

Index

CCTV cameras like this
can be found on street
corners all over the world.